Urgent Plea for Prayer: 31 Days of Prayer

Gail E. Dudley

Copyright © 2017 by Gail E. Dudley

Urgent Plea for Prayer:
31 Days of Prayer
by Gail E. Dudley

Printed in the United States of America

ISBN: 978-0-9752921-9-8

All rights reserved. No part of this document may be reproduced or transmitted in any form, by any means (electronic, photocopying, recording, or otherwise) without the written permission of the author.

Unless otherwise indicated, Bible quotations are taken from Holy Bible, New International Version®, NIV®. Copyright ©1973, 1978, 1984, 2011 by Biblica, Inc.® Used by permission. All rights reserved worldwide.

Scriptures marked NASB are taken from the New American Standard Bible. Copyright © 1960, 1962, 1963, 1968, 1971, 1972, 1973, 1975, 1977, 1995 by The Lockman Foundation.

Scriptures marked ESV are taken from The Holy Bible, English Standard Version. ESV® Permanent Text Edition® (2016). Copyright © 2001 by Crossway Bibles, a publishing ministry of Good News Publishers.

Scriptures marked KJV are taken from the King James Version of the Bible. Public domain.

Scriptures marked AMP are taken from the Amplified Bible. Copyright © 2015 by The Lockman Foundation, La Habra, CA 90631. All rights reserved.

Table of Contents

Introduction v

Day 1	Prepare 7
Day 2	Praise 10
Day 3	You Are My Song! 13
Day 4	Let's Be Available! 18
Day 5	Get Ready to Experience an Encounter with God 20
Day 6	Believe! 23
Day 7	Know Him 25
Day 8	Let's Break It! 29
Day 9	Jesus Loves Me! 30
Day 10	Remove All Distractions! 31
Day 11	Yes, You Can! 33
Day 12	Praise and Worship 35
Day 13	Let's Get to Work! 39
Day 14	Worship 42
Day 15	Stay the Course 43
Day 16	This Is Why We Pray 47
Day 17	You Have Authority! Use It! 48
Day 18	Heed the Warning! Pay Attention! 52
Day 19	Grieve 56
Day 20	Shine 58

Day 21	Wait on the Lord	60
Day 22	Yes	61
Day 23	Stewardship, Prosperity, and Finances	62
Day 24	Pray Differently	65
Day 25	Hold On	69
Day 26	Be Filled … Holy Spirit, Come	71
Day 27	Holistic Prayer Life	78
Day 28	Thirst for God	81
Day 29	Miracles Do Happen	82
Day 30	I Don't Feel Like Praying	85
Day 31	A Call for Action	86

Walk It Out 89

What's Your Story? 89

Prayer Requests 93

Praise Reports 100

Transformational Prayer Coaching 107

Transformational Prayer Experience 109

Prayer Resources 111

Statement of Faith 114

About the Author 117

Booking Information 118

Other Books by Gail 119

Introduction

Welcome to *31 Days of Prayer*.

There is urgency all around us to pray. No longer can we put off until tomorrow what we should do today. It is not by mistake you picked up this book. Today is the day your journey begins for 31 days.

There's an urgency to pray. There's something in the atmosphere that is drawing God's people to pray. Maybe there's an urgency to pray for jobs. Maybe there's an urgency to pray for a solid career path. Maybe there's an urgency to pray for your purpose. Maybe there's an urgency to pray for family relationships. Maybe there is an urgent plea to pray for marriages. It could be an urgent need to pray for your neighborhood and local community. Your financial situation maybe in a downward spiral, which creates an urgency for you to pray. Maybe there's an urgency to pray for your local and state government. Maybe the immediate need for prayer is your federal government.

Whatever the urgency, let us take the next 31 days and pray. Let's make a commitment to pray the moment we sense a drawing in the spirit to lift a name or a situation. As you sit on the subway, drive on the highway, or walk down the street, be aware of your surroundings. As you speak with family and friends, be available to stop and silently pray. As you watch the news or hear a broadcast, be mindful of the tugging on your spirit. It may very well be the Holy Spirit calling you to pray.

Gathering the community in prayer brings about unity and a force to collectively seek the throne of God on behalf of others. When you join in intercession one with another breakthroughs happen, minds are renewed, transformation occurs, people are delivered, healing takes place, lives are changed, and the power of the Lord is with us.

A word of encouragement. You may find that the urgency lifts; however, I would like to encourage you to continue reading each day until you have completed the 31 days. Why? It is a part of the enemy's trick. He lets up long enough for us to stop praying and then he attacks again. Please continue to pray.

This book will become one that is placed on your shelf to read over and over again every time you sense an urgency to pray. Allow this book to be your guide after you have picked up the Bible to read Scriptures.

It will only take 15 minutes per day to work through each day in this book, but it will be worth the investment of time.

You will find throughout the 31 days there may be video or audio links. For ebooks simply click on the link or copy the link to your browser. For print books type the URL in your browser.

Teams of intercessors are available to join you in prayer. At any time if you have a prayer request do not hesitate to send our way. Send to ReadyToPray@gmail.com.

Let's commit to praying and fasting each Wednesday within the 31 days.

We are on this journey together. Are you ready to pray? Let's begin.

DAY 1

Prepare

Let's prepare by putting everything on the table.

You will face some things as you are praying, interceding, and fasting. Please encourage at least one other person to join you in prayer during this time and as you continue your journey of prayer. Think in this way: Praying community. This means as you are praying for someone, be sure to have someone praying for you. As that person is praying for you, be sure to have someone praying for that person and so forth. Praying community means as one person is praying, they too are being covered in prayer.

First Week of Your 31 Days ~

This week:

- Know how to stand, believing and trusting God as you pray.
- Be prepared when you encounter difficulty.
- Put on the whole armor of God. This is a priority in making the decision to stand and to pray.
- Come to an understanding that the only real enemy you as a Christian have is the one who is the enemy of Christ.
- Continue to pray. Push through. We are doing this together.

Focus Scriptures: 2 Corinthians 10:4-5, Ephesians 6:10-19, 2 Kings 6:8-17, 2 Chronicles 20:15-17, Isaiah 43:1-5

Deal with the Concern:

- The moment we begin to pray individually or collectively, seeking God is the same moment things will begin to irritate you, frustrate you, and rob your time. Things will begin to break down in your home. Attacks will appear to come out of nowhere. Recognize that this is only the enemy trying to distract you and take you off course. STAY THE COURSE.
- You will have this thought: "Things were better when I didn't take this time to pray." This thought is a lie from the pit of hell. KEEP PRAYING.

Unless we put on the full armor of God, the devil will try to have his way with us. The enemy wants nothing more than for us to live our life as defeated individuals. The enemy wants us to walk around this world as a victim, not fully knowing who we are as a child of God. His plan is to get us to walk around in defeat, afraid, depressed, oppressed, and to some degree a loser. Remember ... "The prayers of the righteous avails much" (James 5:16).

Let's Deal with the Questions

How can I pray when the moment I make the commitment, get serious, and take time to pray, things appear worst than before? What shall I do to take my stand and put on the full armor of God and intercede

Day 1 – Prepare

on behalf of others and pray for myself, family, and household?

1) We must clothe ourselves in the armor of God.
2) Understand that a stronghold is simply a place of strength. Strongholds represent the area of our mind and patterns of thinking that influence our words, actions, and behaviors. They affect our relationships and cloud and confuse our perceptions of reality.
3) Look past the surface and see with your spiritual eyes the real issue:
   a) the real enemy;
   b) the real distraction;
   c) the real war that is going on.
4) Trust God! Walk in the authority of Jesus.
5) Know who you are and know 'Who' you belong to. His name is JESUS.
6) Pray without ceasing (1 Thessalonians 5:17).
7) Have someone cover you in prayer as you are praying.

The next seven days, be very clear of your kingdom priority (Matthew 6:33). Understand that the struggle for power is the game of the enemy. As Christians in this world, we are called to simply "walk" in the power and the authority of Jesus Christ through love, righteousness, faith, peace, and joy. We know that:

- Jesus has overcome the world (John 16; 1 John 2:13-14; 5:4-5).
- We are more than conquerors (Romans 8:37).
- The gates of hell will not prevail (Matthew 16:18).

DAY 2

Praise

Let's confuse the enemy and begin to **PRAISE!** Throughout this entire day, no matter what may come your way, **PRAISE!**

Seriously, no matter what is going on, even if it's a crisis, begin to praise. Sing songs all day long. Hit the repeat button on your smart phone, in your car, on your tablet, iPod, etc. Dance today! Clap your hands today! Speak Scriptures today! Be a person of praise.

"Praise is an act of intense and intentional personal or corporate worship or acknowledgement by which the virtue and action of the sovereign and omnipotent God are celebrated. We praise God for who He is and all that He has done (1 Chronicles 16:25; Psalm 150:2; Isaiah 25:1, Colossians 3:16-18). Praising God for who He is is called adoration. Praising God for what He does is called thanksgiving. The experience of praising the Lord may be in song or prayer, individually or collectively, spontaneous or planned, originating from the emotions or from the will (Psalm 34:1; 71:6, 14). Sometimes our praise is by necessity sacrificial because of what we are experiencing in the battle (Hebrews 13:15). Failure to praise God is to withhold from God what rightfully belongs to Him. We always have a choice as to what we will do in the seasons of our trial and tribulation. You could: stress out, feel bad, get angry, be miserable, run away, live in denial, try to control, lash out, or **YOU CAN PRAISE THE LORD!**" *(quote from Pastor Kevin Dudley, The Church at North Pointe teaching from "The Fight of Your Life.")*

"However, if you suffer as a Christian, do not be ashamed, but praise God that you bear that name" (1 Peter 4:16).

The Process of Praise That Can Be Experienced Personally and Corporately

- Acknowledge who God is,
- Understand who we are,
- Recognize God's presence,
- Expect God to move,
- Wait on God's response.

How are you going to praise today?

_____
_____
_____
_____
_____
_____

Remember ... don't stop praying and praising. The enemy is not happy with us right now. He will do all he can to distract us and try to take us off course. **STAY THE COURSE.** Keep praying and keep praising.

Need a video to help with your praise? For ebooks click here. For print books place this URL in your browser.

EVERY PRAISE *Hezekiah Walker (video)*
https://youtu.be/UuuZMg6NVeA

DAY 3

You Are My Song!

I hope you had one amazing praise party on yesterday. One thing I do to set the atmosphere is to play music. Oftentimes I find one particular song and set the repeat button. Isn't it interesting that God will deposit a song in your spirit at the exact moment you need something to uplift you out of a space of oppression and depression? I am learning to be obedient to His still, small voice that tugs on me to pay attention. God is amazing. Yes, attacks may come our way from time to time, but it is important to stay focused. We cannot quit now. So let's get started on Day 3.

A couple things to remember as you pray:

- It is important to know and believe Jesus. *Not believe 'in,' but believe Him.*

"I am the Alpha and the Omega," says the Lord God, "who is, and who was, and who is to come, the Almighty" (Revelation 1:8).

- It is important to invite Jesus to come in.

"Here I am! I stand at the door and knock. If anyone hears my voice and opens the door, I will come in and eat with him, and he with me" (Revelation 3:20).

- It is important to come to God with our heart.

Seek His face — acknowledge Christ — and call out to Him, "Abba Father!" It is about praying the Lord's heart and praying what He desires. It is about praying prayers that align with the Word of God. When our heart is lined up with His heart and when we give ourselves totally to God, we pray what He desires us to pray.

As we pray His heart we are able to wrap our minds around this example ~ *(reprinted from Ready to Pray, A Workbook: A Spiritual Journey of Prayer and Worship)*

Think about a symphony orchestra. The most important person in an orchestra is the conductor. The conductor does not play an instrument at all. The conductor's job, at its most basic level, is to indicate the beat of the music. The conductor uses a baton to instruct the entire orchestra. With each movement of the baton, the conductor is instructing with imaginary points that indicates the beat in the bar the orchestra is playing.

Think about Jesus. He is the most important person during your conversation. When your heartbeat begins to line up with His heartbeat, you will find yourself praying what He is praying, "Thy kingdom come, thy will be done." You are now praying what He desires you to pray. You are now focused on His thoughts and His will and His direction and find that your thoughts are no longer as important as before. Your mind is now focused on Christ Jesus.

When you are falling in love with Jesus and becoming more intimate with Him through prayer, you will learn His voice. As the

Day 3 – *You Are My Song!*

conductor, Christ will prepare you. You see, the conductor's role in the orchestra is being responsible for the preparation, the rehearsal, and for making interpretative decisions, such as whether a certain passage should be slow, fast, soft, loud, smooth, aggressive, and so forth. The same could be adopted as you are praying and talking with Jesus. He will speak to you boldly, compassionately, through a whisper, in silence, and will instruct you to be obedient. Through the reading of His Word, you will know to wait patiently, move swiftly, to be still, and so on.

A conductor of an orchestra communicates their decisions both verbally during the rehearsal and during the performance, using different movements, gestures, and expressions. During prayer, you will know what Jesus is communicating with you because you have spent time with Him. You have become more intimate with Him and your heartbeat is now beating with His.

Next, think only about the symphony. There are usually four movements to a symphony. A *sonata*, from the Italian word meaning, "to sound," often is the first movement, sometimes referred to as "sonata form" or "first-movement form." Our prayers should be based upon the conductor, Jesus Christ, and be in concert with Him through intercession.

With a typical symphony, the first movement is a fairly fast movement, weighty in content and feeling. That's where we get the "sonata form." Looking at prayer, when we begin to pray and spend time with the Lord, we are usually in a hurry. We rush through our time with Him because we don't always know what to expect.

The second movement of a symphony will be slow and solemn in character. As we pray, we may find the second time around to be quieter, slower. The pounding of the heart slows down. There's room for silence—you may no longer be in a hurry. You have decided to take your time and watch and pray.

The third movement of a symphony can be interchanged with the second movement. When we pray, we may find ourselves in a hurry in the beginning, but later, get with God and slow down because we are finally resting in His arms.

The fourth movement in a symphony creates the finale. The finale is made up of a variation. A variation movement consists of a theme, usually made up of four- or eight-bar phrases in which the theme is elaborated, developed, and transformed.

Although a symphony may seem difficult in our natural hearing, it's easy to those who are a part of the orchestra. With Christ, we may think this journey of prayer and worship is difficult, but it's a beautiful journey once we line up with Christ as the focus of our time in intercession and prayer with Him.

- Once we are in concert with Jesus Christ, we move into intercession.
- When we pray, even in our weakness, the Holy Spirit is present. Romans 8:26 says, "In the same way, the Spirit helps us in our weakness. We do not know what we ought to pray for, but the

Day 3 – You Are My Song!

Spirit himself intercedes for us with groans that words cannot express."[1]

We are in this together.

YOU ARE MY SONG *by Fred Hammond (video)*
https://youtu.be/0naEf6h931g

Write what God is saying to you at this moment: ____

_____
_____
_____
_____
_____
_____
_____
_____
_____
_____
_____
_____
_____
_____
_____
_____
_____
_____
_____
_____
_____
_____
_____
_____
_____

---

[1] Gail E. Dudley, *Ready to Pray, A Workbook* (Columbus, OH: Highly Recommended International, Inc., 2014), 24-26.

DAY 4

Let's Be Available!

Take time today to be available. Take a few moments and sit in silence. Turn off all the noise. Take time to share your heart with Jesus. Take a deep breath and breathe. Listen to the beat of your heart. Take three minutes and be completely present in the moment.

- Available:

    o to have your heart examined by God,
    o to receive truth from God,
    o to be still and sit quietly and hear the voice of God,
    o as you sit, waiting eagerly and expecting God's answers, and
    o to walk boldly and with authority in the confidence and obedience of Christ.

- Intentional:

    o Search the Scriptures and begin to circle or highlight all prayers in the Bible.
    o Keep a prayer journal and read through it regularly. Put a red line through the request once God has answered.
    o Stay focused on Jesus even when things become challenging. Do not allow yourself to give in to defeat.

Day 4 – Let's Be Available!

- o STAY THE COURSE ~ KEEP PRAYING ~ ASK SOMEONE TO COVER YOU AS YOU ARE PRAYING.

Are you available?
Allow this song to speak to your spirit.

Lord, I am Available to You,
by the Brooklyn Tabernacle Choir.
https://youtu.be/tJznj1a8I1w

Have a prayer request? Please send them to ReadytoPray@gmail.com.

DAY 5

Get Ready to Experience an Encounter with God

"Peter was kept in prison, but the church was earnestly praying to God for him" (Acts 12:5).

King Herod seized Peter during the Feast of Unleavened Bread. He was placed in jail and handed over to four soldiers. There were plans to have him brought before the public after the Passover. Peter was in a bad situation, but the church was praying.

During your 31 days you never know whom you may be praying for. Yes, you may be praying for someone specifically, but I guarantee that you are also praying for individuals you do not know. If we are praying community, our prayers may change from, "Lord, bless my family," to "Lord, bless the community." Someone in the community may need that prayer of blessing at that particular time and because you prayed they were blessed.

As you drive by a school your prayers may be, "Lord, open the mind of my son/daughter to learn and gain knowledge." When praying community your prayer may change to say, "Lord, open the minds of all the students to learn and gain knowledge." Because of your change in prayer many more students' minds around the world may open to learn and gain knowledge. Isn't that beautiful?

As in the Scripture, when we pray, things can happen suddenly! SUDDENLY ... "Suddenly an angel of the Lord appeared and a light shone in the cell. He struck Peter on the side and woke him up. 'Quick, get up!' he said, and the chains fell off Peter's wrists" (Acts 12:7).

Because of your faithfulness. Because you made a commitment to pray. Because people are joining you in prayer ... your SUDDENLY is here. Today experience a God encounter. Today experience a miracle.

Miracles Are an Amazing Event
No Matter How Big or Small

- It's an unexplainable event. It's supernatural.
- It's an intervention that comes unexpectedly, but right on time.
- It's God's divine covering and protection when you cannot see your way out of a situation.
- It's an unexpected answer.
- It's a divine appointment that cannot be explained.
- It's the manifestation of God's presence.

Today you will experience a miracle. You will have a God encounter.

Urgent Plea for Prayer: 31 Days of Prayer

How are you praying today for a 'Suddenly?' _____
_____
_____
_____
_____
_____
_____
_____
_____
_____

What miracle took place for you or for someone you prayed for today? _____
_____
_____
_____
_____
_____
_____
_____
_____
_____
_____
_____
_____

DAY 6

Believe!

- Believe. Deal with any unbelief you may be wrestling with. Ask God to help you with your unbelief (Mark 9:24).
- Forgive. Make sure there is no unforgiveness in your heart. This is the greatest block to answered prayer (Matthew 6:14-15).
- Repent. Go to God and repent of any sin (Matthew 6:14-15).

Jesus says in Mark 11:24-25, "Therefore I tell you, whatever you ask for in prayer, believe that you have received it, and it will be yours. And when you stand praying, if you hold anything against anyone, forgive him, so that your Father in heaven may forgive you your sins."

What are you believing God for today? _____

_____
_____
_____
_____
_____
_____
_____
_____
_____
_____

Are you holding on to any unforgiveness? If so, take a moment and write down what or who you need to forgive. _____

_____
_____
_____
_____
_____
_____
_____
_____
_____
_____

Decide today to forgive and let it go. Repent.

Need someone to come alongside and join you in prayer? Send your prayer request to: ReadyToPray@gmail.com.

DAY 7

Know Him

Let's get real. The first six days have been what I will call a time of 'building.' Now that we are at Day 7, let's deal with our lack of intimacy with God in order to know Him and the beauty of His holiness. We read in 1 Corinthians 1:2 the following, "To the church of God in Corinth, to those sanctified in Christ Jesus and called to be holy, together with all those everywhere who call on the name of our Lord Jesus Christ—their Lord and ours...."

It's one thing to pray; however, it is life altering to pray to God the Father, God the Son, and God the Holy Spirit. There is something peaceful about spending time with Jesus. It is about a deeper relationship and intimacy. It is about understanding His silence as pure intimacy. Here's an example.

As a married woman I can enjoy my husband; our laughter, our date nights and dinner, our watching movies together, our traveling up and down the highway having rich conversations. However, there's something one cannot explain in our togetherness of silence. Sitting in the same room but in silence, truly enjoying the presence of the other. Riding in the car together but in silence, experiencing the joy of just being with one another. Pure intimacy appears in the silence. When you have peace, comfort, and joy in the silence, that is when you'll experience true intimacy. Sometimes you just have to sit there in the silence.

We have been taught that someone is 'mad' or 'angry' with you if they are silent. We have also been taught that silence means someone is having a bad day, or they are depressed, stressed, or facing a challenge. Silence is not negative, as we may have been taught. Thinking of silence as 'bad' could be a lie from the enemy to get you distracted and possibly to frustrate the other person to take them off course. Maybe that person's silence is simply taking in the view of what one may be seeing in the supernatural. One's silence may be their communication that they are at peace with you.

It is in the silence that we can learn of God and truly get to know Him.

Here are a few Scriptures to meditate on:

"Those who know your name will trust in you, for you, Lord, have never forsaken those who seek you" (Psalm 9:10).

"We are destroying speculations and every lofty thing raised up against the knowledge of God, and we are taking every thought captive to the obedience of Christ" (2 Corinthians 10:5, NASB).

"And this is my prayer: that your love may abound more and more in knowledge and depth of insight, so that you may be able to discern what is best and may be pure and blameless until the day of Christ, filled with the fruit of righteousness that comes through Jesus Christ — to the glory and praise of God" (Philippians 1:9-11, NASB).

"Whoever does not love does not know God, because God is love" (1 John 4:8).

Day 7 – Know Him

Know Him. Google "Names of God" and take a name each day the rest of this month and get to know Christ in a more intimate way. Here are few names to get you started:

El Shaddai ~ The All-Sufficient One
El Elyon ~ The Most High God
Jehovah-Nissi ~ The Lord My Banner
Elohim ~ The Creator
Jehovah-Shalom ~ The Lord My Peace
Jehovah-Jireh ~ The Lord My Provider
Jehovah-Raah ~ The Lord Is My Shepherd
Jehovah-Shammah ~ The Lord Is There
Jehovah-Tsidkenu ~ The Lord Our Righteousness
Adonai ~ Lord, Master
El Roi ~ The God Who Sees
Yahweh ~ Lord (Jehovah).

Please note: Everywhere you see Jehovah, you can change it to Yahweh because that is the translation. So instead of saying, "Jehovah-Raah" you can say, "YHWH." Want to understand why I spelled Yahweh that way? Do your research; you will be amazed. You see, praying is about knowing.

By the way (I won't leave you hanging):

Yahweh (YHWH): Comes from a verb that means "to exist, be."

It has been one full week of prayer. How do you feel after reading each day, listening to music, praising God, sitting still, meditating, and of course praying?

_____
_____
_____
_____
_____
_____
_____

Let's get everyone we know praying.

"For the prayers of the righteous avail much" (James 5:16).

"If my people, who are called by my name, will humble themselves and pray and seek my face and turn from their wicked ways, then will I hear from heaven and will forgive their sin and will heal their land. Now my eyes will be open and my ears attentive to the prayers offered in this place" (2 Chronicles 7:14-15).

How do you know and experience God? _____
_____
_____
_____
_____
_____
_____
_____
_____

DAY 8

Let's Break It!

Let us break all the stuff that has caused the bondage in our life.

Some people are unable to move forward until the weight of life has been dismantled. It is time to stop focusing on everyone and everything and begin intentionally focusing on God. STAY THE COURSE. KEEP PRAYING. HAVE OTHERS COVER YOU AS YOU PRAY.

List everything that has kept you distracted from focusing on God and His Word. _____
_____
_____
_____
_____
_____
_____
_____

What steps are you going to take to change your focus? _____
_____
_____
_____
_____
_____
_____

DAY 9

Jesus Loves Me!

"So we have come to know and to believe the love that God has for us. God is love, and whoever abides in love abides in God, and God abides in him" 1 John 4:16 (ESV).

Let's send messages of "LOVE" today. As we continue to pray for one another, may we remember that Jesus has a special love for each one of us individually.

Take time to reflect on the love God has for you. Take time today to search the Scriptures of His love. Take a highlighter and circle each love Scripture.

Take an index card and write, "God loves me!" and place this in a place that you can view regularly.

Have a prayer request? Send to: ReadytoPray@gmail.com.

DAY 10

Remove All Distractions!

Ever find yourself distracted? You start your day with a plan and within the first hour things are offtrack. Cooking, getting your children off to school, fighting a sickness, juggling several projects, reading your Facebook newsfeed, checking Twitter, Instagram, Pintrest, LinkedIn, washing and folding laundry, watching television, and whatever else finds its way into your space.

Here's the truth: We allow these distractions.

When we make a decision to pray, fast, and/or intercede on behalf of another, we will get distracted. I have one question. What are you going to do to stay focused?

Satan would want nothing more than to stop us from praying fervently. People are being healed through our time of prayer. Truth is coming forth. Relationships are mending. People are confessing Christ. We cannot stop praying during times when we have been prompted to pray, and even more so when we sense an urgency to pray.

There have been times during my prayer journey when I have had to stop in my tracks and pray. There is a sense of pressure upon my chest to pray. I have noticed times when my heart will begin to race as I experience an urgency to intercede. There have even been times when I find myself experiencing shortness of breath, sort of like a quickening to stop and pray.

No, I do not always know whom or what I am praying for. All I know is that I have to pray.

It never fails. The moment I have this sort of experience, satan appears with distractions, and sometimes attacks. When we find ourselves in this state we must ... STAY THE COURSE. KEEP PRAYING. HAVE SOMEONE COVER YOU IN PRAYER AS YOU ARE PRAYING.

Please list ways you have been distracted now that you have decided to pray, fast, and intercede on behalf of another. _____

_____
_____
_____
_____
_____
_____
_____
_____
_____
_____
_____
_____
_____
_____
_____
_____
_____
_____
_____
_____

DAY 11

Yes, You Can!

"*I can do all things through Christ who strengthens me*" (Philippians 4:13, NKJV).

This is Day 11 of focused time of praying and interceding on behalf of others and praying for personal requests. It is around this time you may be ready to throw in the towel. As you are praying you are looking for things to get better, but it appears things are intensifying. You are probably saying, "This is too much." "This is too difficult." "I'm growing weary." "I am exhausted!" The list goes on. This is not the time to quit. This is the exact time to keep praying. Most intercessors can relate. You are thinking, "I can't!" BUT God says, "YES, YOU CAN!"
STAY THE COURSE! KEEP PRAYING! And make sure you HAVE SOMEONE COVERING YOU IN PRAYER!
Write out a prayer in the space below.

First, take a moment to be still. Secondly, ask God to come in and sanctify your imagination. Next, find yourself in a place where only you and God reside. Listen for wind. Listen for water, waves hitting rocks. Listen for the quietness of a water fountain. Listen for a fresh breeze. Steady your breathing. Hear your heart beat. Feel God's presence. Smell His scent. Enjoy this space for a little while.

Now write what He says or has shown you. _____

DAY 12

Praise and Worship

Over the last twelve days there has been a commitment to pray. Day 1 was the day of this clarion call to an 'Urgent Plea for Prayer.' Day 2 we talked about praise and how it will confuse the enemy, especially when he wants you to be depressed and oppressed and give up. Day 3 we worshiped, and Day 4 we dealt with being available. Day 5 was our prayer of healing, miracles, and breakthroughs, which led us to Day 6, a day of believing. Each post is designed to build on the other. This is what it's like to make a commitment to a time of prayer, fasting, and intercession.

There's an urgency that draws you to pray. Usually by the evening of the first day you made the commitment to pray, the enemy has begun a battlefield with your mind. This is why it is important to have a time of praise on Day 2. Most individuals are discouraged and need praise to uplift and shift the atmosphere. Praise will do that. It will uplift and shift the atmosphere. Most times this will lead us to worship. It is after our time of worship that we begin to experience healing, miracles, and breakthroughs, and of course, our eyes are supernaturally opened. When our eyes are opened we can begin to see the fruit of our commitment to prayer.

See the progression? This is why it is important to journal each day of this journey. Take a moment and look back over the previous days and see how God has strengthened you and has given you His power to keep pressing. Take a moment and write down what you are experiencing as you look back over the last twelve days. _____

_____
_____
_____
_____
_____
_____
_____
_____
_____
_____
_____
_____
_____
_____
_____
_____
_____
_____
_____
_____
_____
_____
_____
_____

By Day 7 you start to develop a more intimate relationship with Jesus and find you want to know more about Jesus. As you are drawing closer to Christ, He begins to reveal some things about you, your life, and/or the person(s) you are interceding on behalf of. That leads us to pray away the strongholds … praying for bondages to be broken from the person(s) we are praying for, including ourselves. As we begin to see the strongholds breaking, we realize that Jesus loves us. Believe it or not, the enemy now has a laser focus on us more than ever before and he begins to increase his tactics and send distractions our way. All of his biding is to take us off course. This to some degree will start the cycle all over again and this is why we must remind ourselves, "YES, We Can!"

So here we are on Day 12. Today let us combine praise and worship. In combining the two we will also engage in some warfare. Don't allow that to frighten you. The enemy is already defeated in the name of Jesus.

> *"Prayer in spiritual warfare terms is a declaration that we are on Jesus' side. We are a part of His army."* — Dr. Charles H. Kraft

Six Things to Remember As You Pray

1) Intimacy (with Jesus) is the foundation of prayer. You must have a relationship to have intimacy.
2) Authority. Use the authority given to you by Christ. You have the authority.
3) Thanksgiving. Be thankful and express your thanks.
4) Confession. Confess Jesus as Lord. Then confess any unforgiveness.
5) Intercession. This is the act of warfare. NOTE: Evangelism is spiritual warfare.

6) Asking. Ask Jesus for inner healing, emotional healing, healing of relationships.
7) Faith. Hebrews 11:1: "Now faith is the substance of things hoped for, the evidence of things not seen" (KJV).

TRUTH: It's about Jesus. Count it an honor that He chose you to participate with Him in a time of prayer and intercession. *"We are not to be scared but honored"* (Kraft).

Sidenote: *Do you realize you are not the only person praying? Twelve days ago you decided to pick up this book and spend 31 days reading through each day's prompting and praying. That was the day God tapped you on your shoulder or tugged on your heart to take this journey. Not that you have not prayed many days of your life, but this time it is different. Many started this journey the same time as you. However, with the pressure of the enemy and life distractions, some have made the decision to give up (at least for the moment). This is one of the reasons why we answered the call for this time of prayer and instruction to help people STAY THE COURSE and KEEP PRAYING. This is also why it is important to have at least one other person praying for you while you are praying so you may be covered and encouraged.*

Would you like prayer? Send your prayer request to ReadytoPray@gmail.com and our team of intercessors will intercede for the person(s) you have requested prayer for, including yourself.

DAY 13

Let's Get to Work!

It is time for you to do some work on you. In Day 12 you read a list of seven (7). Item number four (4) 'confession,' "… confess any unforgiveness." Today it is time to confess and deal with 'unforgiveness' and 'disobedience.'

Unforgiveness:

Unforgiveness is a major block to our prayers. God gives us the opportunity to influence others; however, we experience difficulty in praying and interceding because of our unforgiveness. God is calling us to partner with Him. This is an honor. Why hold on to unforgiveness towards self and others? Have you ever questioned why your prayers are not being answered? Are you holding unforgiveness in your heart? If you answered, "Yes" to the questions, why not authentically forgive?

Disobedience:

Did you know that when you are in disobedience you are obeying satan? Prayer is warfare. **Hear this: The enemy is excited that you have disobeyed Jesus.** We must sever the ties of disobedience and unforgiveness. God encourages us to participate with Him, and yet many will ignore the call. This is operating in disobedience. You have a choice. Choose to be with

God or be against God. If you choose God, there's one requirement: Obedience. God is calling us to obey Him. When we make the choice (freewill) to disobey, we are saying to God, "I'd rather obey satan." OUCH!

God is calling us to forgive. Making the choice to continue in unforgiveness is disobeying God. Your freedom is in your forgiveness to others and to self. There are times we overload ourselves with guilt and shame. This brings bondage of unforgiveness. We must also remember to forgive self.

Let's deal with guilt and shame.

Shame, guilt, and condemnation are similar in that they all have to do with sin, but different in degree, duration, and scope.

1) Shame is an emotional feeling that at times can be intense, which makes people perceive themselves as less than, insignificant, unacceptable, or damaged. Shame can make you want to go into isolation, hide, disappear, or even want to die.
2) Guilt is the result of recognizing you have done wrong and find it difficult to forgive yourself. You walk around with guilt riding on your shoulders. This guilt will lead you to a bent position in your posture. This guilt usually stems from some particular sin.
3) Condemnation is being judged, convicted, or a verdict being passed down for doing wrong.

Shame is deeper than guilt. It is not based on having done something wrong so much as a pain of being wrong at the core. Shame is more painful than condemnation where the actuality of judgment is mentally apprehended from an outside authority.

Day 13 – Let's Get to Work!

With shame we obviously feel our own evil in vivid self-realization.

The bondage of guilt and shame will weigh you down. Take a moment and list the guilt and shame you continue to wrestle with. _____
_____
_____
_____
_____
_____
_____
_____
_____
_____
_____

Take a moment to list names of individuals you are being called to forgive. _____
_____
_____
_____
_____
_____
_____
_____
_____
_____

Now take the next step and forgive. Forgiveness is important to remove any blockage from praying.

DAY 14

Worship

So many of you worked through unforgiveness and disobedience on Day 13. Let's just worship. God is worthy.

Video: Hillsong Live, I SURRENDER
https://youtu.be/HcnfT4arZtI?list=PLZiE7X6hsxiiuib6htQEgZtZrQ2t4RShp

DAY 15

Stay the Course

The Daniel Fast – Daniel 10:2-11

- Daniel mourned, consecrated himself, or partially fasted over the plight of his people, Israel. This can be noted in Daniel 10:2-11. We are mourning, consecrating ourselves, or partially fasting over the plight of our local church and extended church family, world, nation, state, city, area, universal church, self, family and extended family, and life situations.
- Daniel mourned for three entire weeks, i.e., 21 days. We are setting aside at least one day (Wednesday) throughout our 31 days.
- Daniel abstained from tasty food: i.e., party food, or desserts, meat and wine.

Be sure you drink plenty of water to stay hydrated.

People are hurting. People are struggling. People are seeking clarity. This could be a clarion call for a time of fasting and praying.

Like Daniel you may decide to start and finish a 21-day fast where you abstain from tasty foods such as party food, desserts, fast foods, coffee that includes cream and sugar, meat, and beverages except for water. Or you may engage in a 3-day fast or a 1-day fast. Whatever you sense you need to draw closer to God to hear from Him and have a time of abstaining from food in order to pray, seek, and surrender.

Here's a prayer strategy for this time set aside to be with God without interruptions.

Seek the Lord for His will, guidance, and direction, along with His protection and covering. Pray for the resources you need (financial, skills, etc.). Pray for family, friends, coworkers, your neighborhood, and church. Pray for a clean heart. Pray for forgiveness. Pray for reconciliation. Pray for an outpouring of God's love and direction.

"Write down the revelation and make it plain on tablets so that a herald may run with it. For the revelation awaits an appointed time; it speaks of the end and will not prove false. Though it lingers, wait for it. It will certainly come and will not delay" (Habakkuk 2:2-3).

- Prepare your heart for the fast by praising and worshiping God.
- Begin with prayer to the Lord and repent of any sins.
- Establish a time each day to spend alone with God. Five minutes, ten minutes, twenty minutes, or even a half hour.
- Read your Bible daily.
- Be specific in your request to God.
- Be expectant. Consider keeping a prayer journal to record thoughts, prayers, and answers.
- Be aware of the enemy's strategies.
- Pray for a prayer partner.

Prayer Strategy

Our main focus in calling this fast is to seek the Lord for His will, guidance, and direction, and for His protection and covering. People are wrestling with life. People are frustrated. There's a lot of division between race, political parties, communities, demographics, nationality, etc. Pray for unity. Pray for resources. Pray for families. Pray for reconciliation. Pray for an outpouring of God's love and direction. Pray for healing.

"Then the Lord replied, 'Write down the revelation and make it plain on tablets so that a herald may run with it. For the revelation awaits an appointed time; it speaks of the end and will not prove false. Though it lingers, wait for it. It will certainly come and will not delay'" (Habakkuk 2:2-3).

- Cleanse your heart.
- As you pray remember to praise and worship the Lord.
- Repent of any sins.
- Extend forgiveness.
- Be obedient to the voice of the Lord.
- Spend alone time with God.
- Find a passage of Scripture and spend time reading and journal what the Lord is speaking.
- Make your requests to God.
- Be expectant regarding answers.
- Be aware of the enemy's strategies. Prepare a list of Scriptures to build up your faith during times of testing and struggle.
- **STAY THE COURSE**
- **KEEP PRAYING**
- Get a prayer partner to pray for you and with you, someone you can call when you need strength or feel overwhelmed.

- When you feel temptation to eat what you have decided to give up, or break the fast ... PRAY, read your BIBLE, WORSHIP.

This is an "Urgent Plea for Prayer." Lives are being transformed, prayers are being answered, healing is taking place, relationships are being reconciled, children are returning home, people are gaining employment, financial resources are being released to those who lack, salvation is happening, there's an increase in Bible-based churches, God's anointing is flowing, and we are reaping what we have sowed. Continue to seek the face of the Lord for "what's next" for local churches, communities, missional ministry, government, schools, students, marriages, sickness, pastors, world peace, being watchmen/women as we seek to continue to do ministry.

"The prayers of the righteous avail much" (James 5:16). Keep praying. Keep fasting. **STAY THE COURSE.**

We want to hear from you. Email us at ReadytoPray@gmail.com. Share how the Lord is blessing you during this time. Share how the Lord is speaking to you.

DAY 16

This Is Why We Pray ...

- Because Jesus made prayer His priority. We can make prayer our priority.
- Because Jesus is a prime example of a life lived by prayer that offers relevance, purpose, answers, and most of all, a relationship with God, the Father. Jesus prayed wholeheartedly for every move He made, asking God for guidance, leading, and direction. He prayed prayers of thanks, prayers for healing, prayers for His disciples, and prayers for believers—present and future.
- Because prayer not only establishes a relationship with God, but it is also vital in maintaining our relationship with Him.
- Time spent with God in prayer deepens our knowledge of and relationship with Him.

This is why we pray.

DAY 17

You Have Authority! Use It!

In seeking God, especially when there is urgency, I often hear God reminding me of our authority we have in Him. The question is, "Do we utilize our authority as God calls us to? Or have we abused our authority?"

Below I have listed Scriptures and have shared words I believe we need to hold close to our hearts in seasons of urgency. Each of us should be encouraged to read the Bible, study, and grow an intimate relationship with Christ. Additionally, we should spend time in God's presence and exercise the authority we have been given. Exercising our authority, I believe, will transform nations.

I believe as Scripture tell us, "If my people, who are called by name, will humble themselves and pray and seek my face and turn from their wicked ways, then I will hear from heaven, and I will forgive their sin and will heal their land" (2 Chronicles 7:14). We will begin to see healing, signs, and wonders that were described when Jesus was fully human. But first, we must humble ourselves, and pray.

> *Very truly I tell you, whoever believes in me will do the works I have been doing, and they will do even greater things than these, because I am going to the Father* (John 14:12).

Day 17 – You Have Authority! Use It!

Jesus said, "Whoever believes in me will do the works I have been doing ... even greater things" (John 14:12). In reading the Scriptures we should be seeing greater works. Wrestle with this question: "Why are we not seeing greater works?"

I wonder if we are not confident enough to stand on His promises and utilize the power and authority He has already given to us. Could it be that we have been distracted?

It's important to notice that Jesus did no healing, signs, or wonders before His baptism.

"and the Holy Spirit descended on him in bodily form like a dove. And a voice came from heaven: "You are my Son, whom I love; with you I am well pleased" (Luke 3:22).

It started with the release of the Holy Spirit, *"But you will receive power when the Holy Spirit comes on you"* (Acts 1:8). There's nothing else to do, but receive.

It's time that we take our stand and invoke the following:

1. God's people must humble. This does not mean be silent; it means to humble ourselves under the authority of Jesus.
2. God's people must pray. This is beyond, "Now I lay me down to sleep." It's time to declare and decree, but only after you have humbled yourself.
3. God's people must seek His face. Stop seeking everything else and seek Christ. He's the only one with the answers. He's the only one with

the power. Surrender whatever you're holding on to and seek Jesus.
4. God's people must turn from wicked ways. Repent. Surrender. Forgive. Love.

"When Solomon had finished the temple of the LORD and the royal palace, and had succeeded in carrying out all he had in mind to do in the temple of the LORD and in his own palace, the LORD appeared to him at night and said: "I have heard your prayer and have chosen this place for myself as a temple for sacrifices. "When I shut up the heavens so that there is no rain, or command locusts to devour the land or send a plague among my people, if my people, who are called by my name, will humble themselves and pray and seek my face and turn from their wicked ways, then I will hear from heaven, and I will forgive their sin and will heal their land. Now my eyes will be open and my ears attentive to the prayers offered in this place. I have chosen and consecrated this temple so that my Name may be there forever. My eyes and my heart will always be there" (2 Chronicles 7:11-16).

We are in a season of experiencing floods, endless murders, lack, loss, division, hate, and so much more. Could it be that God is waiting on you and me to fully live into what He has called us to? It's time to truly humble, pray, seek, turn ... then He will hear, forgive, and heal. His eyes will be open and His ears attentive to the prayers we offer. It's not simply praying. There's something we must do. Authority is ours. God desires to have us partner with Him.

Are you using your authority? Ready to see the nations transformed? Walk in your authority. Humble yourself. STAY THE COURSE. PRAY. Ask others to

Day 17 – You Have Authority! Use It!

cover you in prayer. Seek the face of the Lord. Turn from wicked ways. Surrender. Watch and pray. Stop complaining. Stop praying selfishly.

Let us know how you are going to surrender and start walking in your authority. Email me at <u>ReadyToPray@gmail.com</u>.

DAY 18

Heed the Warning! Pay Attention!

Are you paying attention?
Look around you.
What's going on?
God is speaking.
Are you obeying?

Ezekiel 33:1-20 gives us a clear picture. We have been called to pray. Actually we have been called to watch and pray. Every day we are witnessing signs, but we have not acted on what we are seeing. God has given us the authority. The same authority of Jesus. *(Refer back to Day 17 for more information on authority.)*

We have a choice to make. Let's make this personal. YOU have a choice to make. Are you going to stay in your prayer closet and continue to pray, or will you act on what God is revealing to you during your time of prayer?

With intercessory prayer we are called to warn others. Let's look closely at Ezekiel 33.

> *"The word of the Lord came to me: 'Son of man, speak to your people and say to them: "When I bring the sword against a land, and the people of the land choose one of their men and make him their watchman, and he sees the sword coming against the land and blows the trumpet to warn the people, then if anyone hears the trumpet but does not heed the warning and the sword comes and takes their life,*

Day 18 – Heed the Warning! Pay Attention!

their blood will be on their own head" ' " (Ezekiel 33:1-4).

Let's do some inductive study to get a better understanding of what the Scripture is saying.

1. What are you observing?
    - Things will happen. Appoint people to be on the lookout. Not just look out, but also warn others.
    - Boldness to warn.
    - Blow the trumpet and warn the people when you see something coming against the land and God's people.
    - Whoever hears, but does not respond to the warning, it's on them.
2. What is your interpretation? Pull out of the Scripture and not read into the Scripture.
3. How will you apply this Scripture?
    - Watch and pray.

The Scripture continues,

" 'Since they heard the sound of the trumpet but did not heed the warning, their blood will be on their own head. If they had heeded the warning, they would have saved themselves. But if the watchman sees the sword coming and does not blow the trumpet to warn the people and the sword comes and takes someone's life, that person's life will be taken because of their sin, but I will hold the watchman accountable for their blood.' "Son of man, I have made you a watchman for the people of Israel; so hear the word I speak and give them warning from me" (Ezekiel 33:5-7).

Complete the same inductive study method for verses 5-7. What are you observing? _____

_____
_____
_____
_____
_____
_____
_____
_____
_____
_____
_____
_____

What is your interpretation? _____

_____
_____
_____
_____
_____
_____
_____
_____
_____
_____
_____
_____
_____
_____
_____

Day 18 – Heed the Warning! Pay Attention!

How will you apply this Scripture as you pray?

_____
_____
_____
_____
_____
_____
_____
_____
_____
_____
_____
_____
_____

It's time we begin to pay attention and take heed of the warnings. Share the things you are noticing now that you are paying attention. _____

_____
_____
_____
_____
_____
_____
_____
_____
_____
_____
_____
_____

DAY 19

Grieve

As we pray, it is okay to grieve. It is a part of the process. I will never forget hearing my husband and pastor share the following during our Christian Education hour at church, "Christians need space to grieve and feel what we feel, then process what we feel." He continued by saying, "This is grieving both personal and communal. We must express from the deepest part and use words to express." He summarized his teaching by saying, "Acknowledge what you feel and allow yourself to work it out. In working it out ... call it what it is."

"Blessed are those who mourn, for they will be comforted" (Matthew 5:4).

"Godly sorrow brings repentance that leads to salvation and leaves no regret, but worldly sorrow brings death" (2 Corinthians 7:10).

"He will wipe every tear from their eyes. There will be no more death' or mourning or crying or pain, for the old order of things has passed away" (Revelation 21:4).

As you listen to the song by Chris Tomlin, "We Fall Down," [https://youtu.be/7Ge9O_HOKcE] allow yourself to grieve. Feel what you feel and process what you feel. Allow yourself to weep, cry out, and

Day 19 – Grieve

express yourself from the deepest part of your being. Remember, "Jesus wept" (John 11:35).

After listening to this song, write down what you are discerning. _____

_____
_____
_____
_____
_____
_____
_____
_____
_____
_____
_____
_____
_____
_____
_____
_____
_____
_____
_____
_____
_____
_____
_____
_____
_____
_____
_____
_____
_____
_____
_____

DAY 20

Shine

Welcome to Day 20 of Urgent Plea for Prayer. Have you ever awakened to a bright sunshine piercing through your window? I have. So after I am awakened simply by this bright presence that cannot be explained, I find my way down the stairs toward the kitchen. I sit at the table and gaze at the beauty of His holiness, sitting in awe of God as I am consistently reminded of just how amazing He is.

Usually with this sort of glaze it gives a mirrored reflection of the light into the darkness. I find I ask God often, "Lord, what are You speaking?" Many times God does not immediately respond, so I sit in silence. In His time He will reveal to me answers to many questions. When it comes to a glaze that sometimes awaken me from my slumber, He gives me the same answer. He impresses upon me the following, "When we pray there will be times of darkness; however, in the darkness His light will shine forth." Those words always give me calm and comfort. No matter how dark a situation, His light will shine forth!

"For God, who said, 'Let light shine out of darkness,' made his light shine in our hearts to give us the light of the knowledge of God's glory displayed in the face of Christ" (2 Corinthians 4:6).

Day 20 – Shine

There will be times as we intercede on behalf of others that we may face darkness. Just remember, God's light will always cut through the darkness.

Have you ever experienced seeing God's light shine through the darkness as you prayed? Write those times here to refer back to from time to time when you find yourself in darkness. _____

DAY 21

Wait on the Lord

"Jesus, all I want is You." Let's wait on Jesus.
As we pray and intercede there will be times where we must wait. In waiting let us worship.
Waiting is a part of prayer, intercession, and fasting.

Have you experienced a time of waiting? If so, please share how you waited.

_____
_____
_____
_____
_____
_____
_____
_____
_____
_____
_____
_____
_____
_____
_____

Video: William McDowell "Waiting" from his ARISE CD https://youtu.be/MsitmP8hurM plus "All I Want is You" https://youtu.be/ww3IYqCOaxU?list=RDMsitmP8hurM

DAY 22

Yes

Let's ask God, "What am I to do?"

What if He replies, "Say 'YES' to everything I'm asking you to do"?

As individuals who have this urgency to pray, it is time to get into the posture of 'yes' and fully surrender our will to the Lord's will. What does that look like? It's no longer fighting His will.

As we are nearing the end of our 31 days you may be experiencing many different feelings. A part of you may want to resist praying because over the last several days you have been on a roller-coaster of feelings. Crying. Frustrated. Sense of loneliness. Burdened. Praise. Worship. Silence. However, through it all you still sense this urgency to pray. Say, "Yes!" Tell God that you will take time beyond these 31 days to pray whenever He prompts you to pray. Tell God that you will sacrifice time to intercede on behalf of others.

God wants us to partner with Him. He's calling us to partner with Him. Will you join me and others in saying "Yes" to Jesus?

Write a "Yes" commitment to Jesus. _____
_____
_____
_____
_____
_____

DAY 23

Stewardship, Prosperity, and Finances

First fruits.

"Honor the Lord with thy substance, and with the first fruits of all thine increase: so thy barns be filled with plenty, and thy presses shall burst forth with new wine" (Proverbs 3:9-10, KJV).

Throughout the Bible, we see God having a lot to say about finances. He desired to be involved and was involved with Abraham's finances, and He desires and wants to be involved in our finances. Oftentimes we find ourselves distracted to pray because we are thinking about our finances. As intercessors we must push past this and trust God with our money, no matter if it's $2 or $2,000, or more.

Here's the truth. As believers we must understand some basic principles. You cannot be a person filled with greed and truly prosper. We can follow Abraham and his prosperity to gain some understanding.

1. Be rich in your relationship with Jesus.
   - *"And Abram was very rich in cattle, in silver, and in gold"* (Genesis 13:2, KJV).
2. Listen and obey God.
   - Abram listened to, and obeyed God (Genesis 12:1-4).

3. Honor God.
    o Abram honored God, who prospered him and his offspring (Genesis 12:7).
4. Be generous. Sow seeds. Avoid contention.
    o Abram was extremely generous, and avoided conflict (Genesis 13:5-9).
5. Be kind and compassionate. Look out for the well-being of others.
    o Abram was compassionate toward others and looked out for one another (Genesis 18:24-33).

"He who gives to the poor will not want, but he who hides his eyes (from their want) will have many a curse" (Proverbs 28:27, AMP).

The motive of your heart must be pure, to bless others, and establish God's covenant. Speak life, not death. When you speak negatively (death) about your financial situation, you have what you say and believe. You may believe in both a tithe and an offering and give accordingly; however, if you speak death to your tithe and offering, you will reap the death you speak of your finances. For example: Let's say you tithe and give an offering, work hard, and pray for your finances regularly. But as you continue to struggle financially and witness your bills growing, not able to make ends meet, and the debt collectors calling, you start speaking words such as, "I'm poor. I'm broke. I do not have any money." You are speaking negatively and contrary to God's Word. Therefore, it is possible that you may stay in debt, struggling to make ends meet.

There may be an urgency to pray for your finances. You want to understand that your words have power.

<u>Words are powerful</u>, *but God's Word is full of power.* When you line up your words with God's Word you will witness your circumstances beginning to change and line up with His will for your life.

I have had many people who have been praying email us saying it's hard to pray when you are faced with financial debt. I'm not sure how God is going to move in your particular situation; however, I'm lead to pray this prayer for all of you reading this book. Will you pray with me? *(Before you pray ... remember there's nothing magical about this prayer. Prayer is not about magic or a disillusion, but about the power and the authority we have in Jesus as believers.)*

> Father, we love You. We bless Your Name and honor You. Lord, based upon the authority You have given to each of us, we pray in the Name of Jesus all our debt paid completely. In the name of Jesus we speak to our debt (individually and collectively) to be paid and be gone right now, never to return. With the authority of the Holy Spirit we speak, "Debt you must dematerialize and cease to exist." We declare that our debts, medical bills, mortgages, loans, and notes are paid in full, cancelled, and/or dissolved. Father, please forgive us for the debt we made innocently or knowingly. We ask that You bless us and give us Your wisdom to be better stewards over our finances now that You have allowed us to be free from our past debts. We pray this in the name of Jesus with thanksgiving. Amen.

God's Word is living and active (Hebrews 4:12).

DAY 24

Pray Differently

"The effectual fervent prayer of a righteous man availeth much" (James 5:16, KJV).

Pray for the destructive plan of the enemy to be canceled in the name of Jesus.

Pray for cancellation of all of the demonic assignments against God's children.

Pray for cancellation of individuals having suicidal thoughts.

Pray for individuals who are experiencing mental illness.

Pray for the atmosphere to change in areas filled with darkness.

Pray liars are transformed in the name of Jesus.

Pray for individuals seeking divorce to be moved to reconcile with their spouse.

List out areas you want to see changed. _____

Day 24 – Pray Differently

Let's pray:

Lord Jesus, we come to You praying and pleading the blood of Jesus and Psalm 91 over, through, around, and about each of these prayer requests. We pray for Your covering upon each person's spirit, mind, will, emotions, ego, imaginations, thoughts, physical beings, all spiritual and natural doors and openings coming into their life, properties, the atmosphere above and around including each persons home and properties, their workplaces, all in the name of Jesus.

Lord, with the authority You have given to us we bind, render, and command satan and all his followers not to manifest themselves in the lives (individuals) of the requests listed and those unspoken. All evil spirits and their effects are rendered powerless and harmless, unable to come back through any opening to any of us, our presence, the presence of our family, the presence of our homes, cars, lands, properties, workplaces, churches, this day and all the days of our life, in the name of Jesus.

Father, we ask You, according to John 14:13-14, to loose now Your angels around each of us. No weapon formed shall prosper. Please release Your angels to stand guard around us, and set a hedge of protection around all intercessors and their families as we are interceding on behalf of others.

Lord, please continuously keep out all demonic spirits from all of us and those we are praying for. Lord, those seeking abundance financially, we ask that You bless right now. May they be better stewards of their resources than they were previously. Lord, those seeking employment or for their business to succeed, give unto them their request. Lord, those seeking to succeed in higher learning Lord, bless their memory and their skills, and their knowledge to propel forward with boldness.

Lord, those who are tired, please give them Your strength right now, in the name of Jesus. Lord, those seeking healing in their marriage, bless now. Lord, those who need to seek assistance, break their pride and allow them to humbly seek help. Lord, for those who are seeking healing, we ask You to heal immediately. Lord, for those who are lost and confused, give to them Your peace and comfort. Lord, we pray for every family who mourns the lost of their love ones. Lord, we are praying for every entrepreneur who is a believer to witness the manifestation of Your presence and to see their labor bear much fruit and gain an overflowing in their profit margin immediately. May they witness their business gain immediate increase of customers, clients, investors, and finances right now, in the name of Jesus.

Lord, we pray for healing to take place not only in Charleston, but around the world were terrorism and racism is taking place. For children who have ran away from home, guide them back safely unharmed. God, wherever there is abuse in the homes, may it cease immediately, in the name of Jesus. For all who are held captive in sex slavery, may they be released and their abuser be brought to justice.

Lord, may each person reading this and commenting receive victory today, in the name of Jesus. This is our prayer. Touch us now, and Lord, hear our prayers. Amen.

We seal this prayer right now in the name of Jesus. We collectively agree and say, "AMEN! in the name of Jesus!"

The prayers of the righteous avail much! (James 5:16)

Desire a team of intercessors to join you in prayer? Send your prayer request to: ReadyToPray@gmail.com.

DAY 25

Hold On

Whatever you do, hold on. Keep praying. **STAY THE COURSE**. I have experienced that when you answer the call of God to pray, you will experience a mighty move of God because of your faithfulness.

We have been praying for 25 days. We have been diligent, steadfast, and unmovable. We have been tried, frustrated, and at times perplexed. We have been pressed, pushed, but we have remained prayerful. Think about wind blowing, and a tree. Imagine as the wind blows, so does the Holy Spirit. As I illustrate the tree, the blowing wind, and leaves, imagine a wind that practically takes a tree to the point of almost breaking, but it bounces back to a straight position.

This illustration is no different than our life with Jesus. Trouble may come. Things may be shaken. At times it may seem gray and hopeless, but with God the Author and Finisher of our faith we are in great hands. Get ready for your suddenly. You've stood this test and prayed, and interceded on behalf of others. You never gave up. Your change in season is approaching. The shaking you are experiencing is just a prelude to the overflowing of God's blessing that is upon you. Be filled! Hold on! **STAY THE COURSE!** KEEP PRAYING! Your greater is here. Now receive!

"Suddenly a sound like the blowing of a violent wind came from heaven and filled the whole house where they were sitting. They saw what seemed to

be tongues of fire that separated and came to rest on each of them. All of them were filled with the Holy Spirit and began to speak in other tongues as the Spirit enabled them" (Acts 2:2-4).

DAY 26

Be Filled ... Holy Spirit, Come

Old Testament ~ The Hebrew word for Spirit is **Ruwach**, meaning wind or breath. The wind like the Spirit of God is unseen and active.

New Testament ~ The Greek word for Spirit is **Punuma**, which like the Hebrew word is derived from the meaning of wind or breath.

Questions to ponder:

What are your thoughts of how the Holy Spirit moves in your life? _____
_____
_____
_____
_____
_____
_____
_____
_____
_____
_____
_____
_____
_____
_____

Do you flow in the Holy Spirit or do you resist the Holy Spirit? Explain. _____
_____
_____
_____
_____
_____
_____
_____
_____
_____

Have you experienced the Holy Spirit as Comforter or Helper? Explain.
_____
_____
_____
_____
_____
_____
_____
_____
_____
_____
_____
_____
_____
_____

Day 26 – Be Filled ... Holy Spirit, Come

"All of them were filled with the Holy Spirit and began to speak in other tongues as the Spirit enabled them" (Acts 2:4).

"In him the whole building is joined together and rises to become a holy temple in the Lord. And in him you too are being built together to become a dwelling in which God lives by his Spirit" (Ephesians 2:21-22).

How can you apply the two Scriptures to your life so that you may experience the Holy Spirit? Please take your time and read Acts 2:1-13 and write your thoughts.

_____
_____
_____
_____
_____
_____
_____
_____
_____
_____
_____
_____
_____
_____
_____
_____
_____
_____
_____
_____
_____
_____
_____

Say these words if you truly would like this to take place in your life ~

I want (desire, long, thirst, hunger) to be filled beyond satisfaction.

Words from Watchman Nee ~ *"Let us not forget that the greatest means of edification is not prayer, though that restores us; it is not reading the Word, though that refreshes us; it is not attending meetings and listening to the messages, though this does comfort and encourage us. The greatest means of edification is the discipline of the Holy Spirit in our lives. Like nothing else, this will build us up in strength to be able to minister to others."*[2]

More questions to ponder:

Looking over your life, how can you be filled beyond satisfaction?

---

[2] Watchman Nee, *Secrets to Spiritual Power, From the Writings of Watchman Nee*, compiled by Sentinel Kulp (New Kensington, PA: Whitaker House, 1998), 135.

Day 26 – Be Filled ... Holy Spirit, Come

What's hindering you from being filled beyond satisfaction? _____

Tired of running on empty? _____

List any fears you may have of being filled with the Holy Spirit. What do you need to overcome your fears? _____

_____
_____
_____
_____
_____
_____
_____
_____
_____
_____
_____
_____
_____

In a time of prayer and meditation express your desire for the Holy Spirit to come upon you. He will come. All you have to do is ask.

The Holy Spirit dwells ~

- Holy Spirit gives people life
- Holy Spirit dwells in your as life
- Holy Spirit falls upon His people as power.
- Be filled (John 7:37-39)

Lord Jesus, breathe on us Your Holy Spirit. Thank You Lord, for hearing our prayer. We lift up our hands to You, Jesus, worshiping and praising Your Holy name and worshiping and praising You in the Spirit. We give thanks, praise, and glory to You, completely surrendering ourselves to You. Fill our cup, Lord. Fill us with Your Holy

Day 26 – Be Filled ... Holy Spirit, Come

Spirit. Lord God we thank You that You have granted us out of the rich treasury of Your glory to be strengthened with Your mighty power in our inner being by the Holy Spirit. Oh Lord, how excellent is Your name!

Jesus, we ask that You would dwell in our hearts that we may be rooted deep in love and founded securely on love. We ask that we may have the power and strength to grasp with all the saints how deep and wide Your love is (Ephesians 3:16-18). Lord, we come boldly asking for Your gift of Your Holy Spirit. So we ask You, Lord, to baptize and fill us in and with Your Holy Spirit, just as You filled Your disciples and all who were in the upper room on the day of Pentecost.

Heavenly Father, we want to be disciples of Jesus, filled with the Holy Spirit, just as Your disciples were. We will surrender to Your will and be obedient to all You call us to do. Lord, we don't want anything to block us from receiving this gift of Your Holy Spirit from us; therefore, we authentically forgive all those who have ever caused us pain, trauma, shock, harm, rejection, or shame, and we ask You to forgive them. Lord, forgive us of our trespasses and for holding a judgment against others.

Now Lord, please fill us to overflowing with Your Holy Spirit. We desire to experience You in an amazing, beautiful, and powerful way, remembering to give You all the glory. In the name of Jesus we pray. Amen.

We hope you prayed this prayer with us. Be filled!

Remember to send your prayer request to ReadytoPray@gmail.com and our team of intercessors will be praying for all requests.

DAY 27

Holistic Prayer Life

Prayer is a conversation with God. It's going to God with your heart and coming away with His. Prayer is giving your entire self: mind, will, physical being, and emotion. One could say prayer is much like exercising and eating healthy. You really cannot do one without the other. To some degree they go hand in hand.

I returned to a healthy lifestyle after years of being what I believe was living an unhealthy lifestyle. I started experiencing healthy results of waking early, being alert, the fog in my mind was cleared, I have unbelievable energy, my skin looked healthy, my hair was no longer looking gray or thin, and I felt a sense of renewed confidence and strength. I experienced amazing results! I felt so wonderful I started back to exercising by walking around the neighborhood. As I walked around the neighborhood I started praying for every person and home I was passing. There are times while walking I will discern a need to stop and pray for a moment. I have actually cried while walking pass certain homes. I call this, "Prayer Walking."

I recall one morning when I felt too exhausted to walk although I had eight hours of sleep. There was an urgency to push myself to walk. I took a moment to stand outside of my front door and prayed. I asked God, "What's the urgency? What are you speaking, God?" He didn't answer me, but He led me to walk a different direction. I ended up at a house I was led to stop and pray for a few weeks earlier. There was a 'for sale' sign in the front yard, and police cars lined the driveway. I learned there was some domestic abuse and was told several weeks ago the wife had locked herself up in an area trying to get away from her husband. I am unsure if it was the same day or not. Regardless, there was urgency. God used me just like He uses you to stop and pray.

I love to swim. I used to race competitively in my younger years and returned to swimming laps. I usually swim 100 laps within one hour. One morning I was prompted to pray as I swam. At one point I felt heaviness in my spirit. As soon as I made it to the wall to stop and breathe I saw several lifeguards jump in the water. The area I swim is for experienced lap swimmers so I was confused as to what was going on. A one-time Olympic swimmer was having difficulty swimming and was beginning to drown.

This is why we answer when God calls. We discern the urgency. There are times we will be drawn to pray. We may be in the area of the urgent need or we may be thousands of miles away. Our call is to be obedient in this season of urgency.

Here's the word for today ~

Holistic health can be difficult and exhausting at times. We may feel like quitting. We may quit. We may readjust some things. We may not give it our all. We may get offtrack. However, when we get offtrack we must begin again somewhere. Sometimes prayer will take everything you have. The key is not to quit. We must **STAY THE COURSE. KEEP PRAYING.**

There are times when we will want to say, "Forget it!" Bottom line, in this season we cannot quit. With praying and interceding on behalf of others, one must have the mind-set that we cannot throw in the towel. We may not be able to give ten minutes to prayer one particular morning, but maybe the next day we can. We may not have the luxury to sit at home in our secret place to pray. That's all right. Just pray. We may become tired and weary at times. No problem. Remember to have someone covering you in prayer while you are praying for others.

Pray takes work. Just like holistic health. To stand in the gap interceding on behalf of another means we must sleep well, exercise regularly, eat healthy, clear our mind, incorporate strength training, and even take days of rest. Jesus rested. We too must rest.

DAY 28

Thirst for God

"Come near to God and he will come near to you. Wash your hands, you sinners, and purify your hearts, you double-minded. Grieve, mourn and wail. Change your laughter to mourning and your joy to gloom. Humble yourselves before the Lord, and he will lift you up" (James 4:8-10).

Two questions we must ponder ~

1) Have you ever had a thirst for God?
2) Are you currently thirsty?

Five points to wrestle through when we find ourselves in a place of brokenness:

1. Submit yourself fully to God
2. Draw near to God
3. Purify your heart
4. Grieve
5. Humble yourself

DAY 29

Miracles Do Happen

Miracles are not solely works of possibility or familiar answers to prayer. Miracles is defined in the dictionary as, "An event that cannot be explained by the known laws of nature and is therefore attributed to divine intervention." Miracles as displayed in the Bible are:

- Elijah praying for fire on the altar (1 Kings 18:23-24)
- The woman with the issue of bleeding (Mark 5:21-24)
- Jairus' twelve-year-old daughter (Mark 5:36-42)
- The woman bent for eighteen years (Luke 13:10-13)
- Lazarus (John 11:38-44)
- The lame man of thirty-eight years (John 5:1-9)

We can also have ...

- Calming of the sea (Matthew 8)
- The blind man healed (Matthew 9)
- The man with the withered hand (Matthew 12)
- The feeding of the multitude (Matthew 14)

How Can We Expect the Miraculous?

Miracles, such as the healing of the woman who was bleeding for twelve years, come by faith. She had faith enough to take a risk and touch the hem of Jesus' garment. She had faith to believe that if she could simply touch the hem, she would be made well. She did not have a formula and she did not perform some sort of ritual. She simply had a little faith. Jesus said, if you have faith even as small as a mustard seed, you can tell your mountain (obstacle, hindrance, or problem) to move and nothing will be impossible for you (Matthew 17:20) ~ *as long as it lines up with the will of the Lord.*

How Shall I Pray?

If praying for the miraculous or praying to intercede on behalf on another we must ...

- Look to God, the author and the finisher of our faith, asking Him to have His way. Seek God regarding the situation. Pray and say to God, "Thy will be done."
- Ask God what He is speaking.
- Once you ask, wait on Jesus to respond. Ask God to give you revelation knowledge.
- Study the Word of the Lord both day and night. Pray and seek God's will through reading His word.
- Believe God.
- Experiencing the miraculous is not manipulating God.

How will you pray when a miracle is needed? _____

How much faith do you have when praying for the miraculous for yourself or for someone else? Please explain. _____

DAY 30

I Don't Feel Like Praying

Have you ever been at a point where you just didn't feel like praying? It wasn't that you could not pray; it was more that you didn't feel like it. I've been there many times.

There are times that I am so caught up in my stuff, my selfish ways, in my situation and challenges that I don't feel like praying.

I asked myself the other day, "What if God didn't feel like talking to me?" There's a thought. It's a little like praise. God does not make me praise Him, but there are times that I just have to. I don't have to, but I have to. If I don't, I just won't feel right.

This is the same with prayer. You ought to pray to Christ every day as often as you can to stay in constant communion with Him. And sometimes it has to be a sacrifice of sleep, talking on the telephone, or hanging out with family and friends. You can't afford not to do it. It may be hard, but it is something we must do in order to know the ways of our Savior Jesus Christ.

We often make praying complicated. We think we must use fancy words, long sentences, sound a certain way, etc. NO—simply bowing our heads and saying the name of Jesus is prayer. Simply saying "thank you" is prayer. Saying "Father, forgive me" is prayer. Waking in the morning and saying "Good morning, Jesus" is prayer.

Even when one does not feel like it—we should pray. Hello Papa! I bless Your name!

DAY 31

A Call for Action

"When this had dawned on him, he went to the house of Mary the mother of John, also called Mark, where many people had gathered and were praying. Peter knocked at the outer entrance, and a servant girl named Rhoda came to answer the door. When she recognized Peter's voice, she was so overjoyed she ran back without opening it and exclaimed, 'Peter is at the door!'" (Acts 12:12-14).

Setting the Stage

On the other side of town the church was praying at the house of a wealthy widow of Jerusalem named Mary, who was the mother of John, also called Mark. She owned a large house in the city.

They were praying for Peter.

They were in a time of intercession.

Meet Rhoda.

Rhoda is a young servant girl who was full of joy and gladness. She was learning and growing. Based upon Scripture, she was in a time of intercession with the others.

As they were praying, Rhoda hears a knock at the door!

It's clear from the Scriptures that no one else heard the knock, but Rhoda!

Day 31 – A Call for Action

I can imagine Rhoda getting up from off her knees, going towards the door.

Scripture tells us that she recognized Peter's voice.

She got excited, but did not open the door.

Have you ever been so close to your miracle that you got too excited and forgot to open the door?

Stop shouting about it and OPEN THE DOOR!

Rhoda could have fallen into believing she was crazy and thought she heard something, but did not … NO … she kept saying, "Peter's at the door!"

The "thing," "the person" we've been praying about is at the door.

Prayer had done what it was designed to do. Now walk out of faith and open the door!

Here's our problem. Oftentimes we keep praying for something when the prayer has been answered.

You'll miss what God has for you if you miss the knock at the door.

> *"I stand at the door and knock! If any man hear my voice, and open the door. I will come in to him, and will sup with him"* (Revelation 3:20, KJV).

We would love to hear from you about your prayer journey.

Thank you for taking this journey with us.

Remember … your help comes from the Lord.
Keep praying and continue to intercede
on behalf of others.

Lives were changed because of your faithfulness to
pray with us during this time.

Whatever you do …

STAY THE COURSE. KEEP PRAYING.

*May the Lord bless you greatly. May His loving arms wrap around you to give you a peace and a comfort. May Jesus wipe every tear that comes from your eyes. May Jesus give you strength to stand and to continue to stand. May God's supernatural power sustain you this day and every day hereafter. May you feel God's love everlasting, and may His presence always be with you. May all your prayers that are aligned with God's will come to you right now, in the name of Jesus. May you live your life in abundance. May God bless you with His wisdom. May you experience greatness and share your love and life with others to glorify God. May God open every door, and may all your requests be manifested right now, in the name of Jesus, because of your faithfulness on this journey.
In Jesus' name. Amen.*

Walk It Out

What's Your Story?

My name is _____ and this is my story.

_____

_____

_____

_____

_____

_____

_____

_____

_____

_____

_____

_____

_____

_____

_____

_____

Walk It Out

Prayer Requests

Urgent Plea for Prayer: 31 Days of Prayer

Prayer Requests

Prayer Requests

Prayer Requests

Praise Reports

Praise Reports

Praise Reports

Praise Reports

Transformational Prayer Coaching

Transformational prayer coaching is where your healing begins at a deeper level. Transformational prayer coaching is where you decide to clothe yourself with strength. Transformational prayer coaching is the place you decide to shake off the dust. Transformational prayer coaching is the place you rise up. Transformational prayer coaching is the place you begin to sit up straight. Transformational prayer coaching is the place you choose to remove the chains from around your neck. Transformational prayer coaching allows you to connect with your redemption.

This in-depth coaching will begin to pull back the Band-Aid of your wounds that you have nursed and kept protected. These wounds are deep-seated suffering and grief that has held you captive with reoccurring emotional shock. You have been thirsting for healing, but the moment a face, a name, or an event enters your mind you find the wound intensifies. This is not what happened to you; it's what remains unprocessed within you.

People are experiencing internal bleeding. People have been deeply cut to the core in some cases. People are wounded. It is time to deal with your wounds. Here's some truth. The longer you stay in the state you are in, the longer it will take you to accomplish all the Lord has for you.

Today you get to choose. Yes. It really is a choice. It is in your hands. You get to choose your path. Today is your opportunity to choose the path towards freedom. If you are interested in Transformational Prayer Coaching, contact info.gaildudley@gmail.com.

Transformational Prayer Experience

In our culture today believers inevitably find themselves living their lives based upon false beliefs, very often unaware of the many harmful influences that have shaped and continue to hold us captive. In order to experience a life of truth, it is absolutely critical to know the truth. God's truth is what sets us free! Many people have the desire to know the truth, but are unsure how to connect and apply God's truth.

Just as we do today, the woman in Genesis 3 fell into the serpent's trap, but God gives us all that we need to overcome the lies. During this transformational weekend participants will gain insight that will help to strengthen and inspire us in our walk with the Lord. If you desire inner healing and a deeper walk with Christ, this weekend is for you.

We will start the weekend on Friday at 1:00 p.m. in a time of prayer, instruction, and inner healing, followed by quiet time. Saturday morning beginning at 9:30 a.m. we will identify the lies that have been spoken into our life and replace those lies with the truth by asking, 'Who Told You That?' The second session on Saturday, 'Ready to Change My Name,' will position us for transformation.

Our weekend will conclude at 2:00 p.m. with small-group instruction that will equip participants to grow deeper in their lives.

Sample Weekend Schedule

Friday ~

    1:00 p.m. ~ Gathering
    1:30 p.m. ~ The Foundation
    2:00 p.m. ~ Prayer Instruction
    3:00 p.m. ~ Inner Healing Experience
    4:00 p.m. ~ Debrief
    5:00 p.m. ~ Time Alone
    6:00 p.m. ~ Dinner on your own

Evening ~ Journal & Reflect

Saturday ~

Breakfast:

    9:30 a.m. ~ Exposing the Lies
    11:00 a.m. ~ Move into Your Future
    12:00 p.m. ~ Lunch on your own
    1:00 p.m. ~ Small-Group Instruction
    2:00 p.m. ~ Commissioning

Look for scheduled Transformational Prayer Weekend experiences on the website: www.GailDudley.com or contact Gail Dudley to book one for your small group, retreat, or church: info.gaildudley@gmail.com.

Prayer Resources

Suggested Books on prayer:

Ready to Pray by Pastor Gail Dudley
A Journey to Victorious Praying by Bill Thrasher
  (Moody Publishers)
Developing a Prayer-Care-Share Lifestyle
  (HOPE Ministries)
Fresh Wind, Fresh Fire by Jim Cymbala
Intercessory Prayer by Dutch Sheets
I Told the Mountain to Move by Patricia Raybon
  (SaltRiver)
Learning to Pray Through the Psalms by James W. Sire
  (InterVaristy Press)
The Power of a Praying Woman by Stormie Omartian
  (Harvest House Publishers)
Pray with Purpose, Live with Passion by Debbie
  Williams (Howard Books)
Prayer by Richard J. Foster
  (HarperCollins Publishers)
Prayer 101: Experiencing the Heart of God
  by Warren Wiersbe (Cook Communications)
Praying God's Word by Beth Moore
  (Broadman & Holman Publishers)
Praying with Women of the Bible by Nancy Kennedy
  (Zondervan)
Possessing the Gates of the Enemy by Cindy Jacobs
Prayer Shield by C. Peter Wagner
What Happens When Women Pray
  by Evelyn Christensen
  (Cook Communications)

Spurgeon on Prayer & Spiritual Warfare
    by Charles Spurgeon
Disciple's Prayer Life
    by T.W. Hunt & Catherine Walker
How to Hear from God by Joyce Meyer
Possessing the Gates of the Enemy by Cindy Jacobs
Prayers that Avail Much
    by Germaine Copeland World Ministries, Inc.
Beyond the Veil by Alice Smith
Intercessory Prayer by Dutch Sheets
Prayer Shield by C. Peter Wagner
Fasting by Jentezen Franklin
A Hunger for God by John Piper
Intimacy with the Almighty by Charles R. Swindoll

Suggested DVD Series on Prayer:

When God's People Pray by Jim Cymbala

Suggested Study Bibles:

The Power of a Praying Woman Bible (NIV)
    by Stormie Omartian
    (Harvest House Publishers)

Suggested Workshops:

The 5-Hour Journey of Prayer Instruction is a one day/5-hour journey of prayer instruction designed to equip individuals, groups, and churches that desire to go deeper in their prayer journey as well as to be effective and impactful during prayer gatherings. For details of future conferences, please visit the website: www.GailDudley.com.

Prayer Resources

Ministry in Motion Ministries founder Gail Dudley is available to bring this workshop to you, sowing 10 percent of the profit back into your ministry or church. The cost per person for the conference is $75.00 per person (non-refundable). The cost includes the 215-page workbook. The cost of lunch is not included.

Suggested Websites on Prayer:

http://www.teachmetopray.com/
    (free 52-week online prayer school)
http://www.globaldayofprayer.com/
http://www.presidentialprayerteam.org/
http://www.prayinglife.org/
http://www.allaboutprayer.org/

Suggested Bible Studies on Prayer:

Boldly Asking by Aletha Hinthorn
    (Beacon Hill Press of Kansas City)
Connecting with God from Stonecroft Ministries
Disciple's Prayer Life: Walking in Fellowship with God
    by T.W. Hunt & Catherine Walker
    (LifeWay Church Resources)
Prayer: An Adventure with God by David Healey
    (InterVarsity)

Statement of Faith

GOD

We believe in one God, existing as three persons; Father, Son, and Holy Spirit, is the loving Creator of all that is, eternal and good, knowing all things, having all power, and desiring and inviting covenant relationship with humanity *(Matt. 28:19; 1 Tim. 1:17; Heb. 1:1-3; 9:14)*.

JESUS CHRIST

We believe in our Lord Jesus Christ, God manifest in the flesh. He alone is the Savior and Lord, the Son of God and God the Son, born of a virgin, the perfect example of humanity, crucified for the sin of the world, raised on the third day and who lives forever to make intercession for us. We confess the absolute lordship and leadership of the risen Jesus Christ, who is the Son of God and God the Son, and our soon-returning King *(Col. 1:15-20; Col. 2:9; John 1:1; Gal. 4:4; Phil. 3:10)*.

THE HOLY SPIRIT

We believe in God the Holy Spirit. At the point of salvation a person receives the Holy Spirit. We receive the abiding presence, peace, and power of the Holy Spirit in every believer as sufficient and necessary for normal Christian living *(Acts 1:8; Eph. 2:22; Rom. 8:9-30)*.

SCRIPTURE

We believe in the Holy Scripture as originally given by Christ, divinely inspired, and revealed by

God, unchanging and infallible Word of God, correct doctrine, the complete truth, authority, and relevance of every promise, provision, God's story of love and redemption (John 1:1; 2 Pet. 1:19-21; 2 Tim. 2:15; 3:16).

SALVATION

We believe in the salvation of the lost and sinful people by grace alone, through faith alone, in Christ alone. We accept the grace of God through the finished work of Jesus on the cross as victory for eternal and abundant life, and we maintain spiritual sonship and citizenship in the present and future Kingdom of God *(Rom. 10:9-10; Eph. 2:8-9).*

UNITY of THE BODY OF CHRIST

We believe in the unity of the Body of Christ and in the Spirit. Unity comprised of, teaching, prayer, fellowship, breaking of bread, meeting ministry needs, praise and worship, people being saved *(Eph. 4:1-6; Acts 2:42-47).*

HUMANITY

We celebrate the sacredness and uniqueness of every person as wonderfully created in the image of God and according to God's sovereign will, called to lives of Christlikeness through personal holiness, honor, and humility *(Heb. 2:6-12).*

SIN and EVIL

We acknowledge our sin and brokenness but refute anything that seeks to deny, discourage, or destroy the life that Jesus offers to all believers *(2 Cor. 4:1-18).*

MINISTRY

We believe that we should go, preach, and make disciples of Jesus Christ. We believe that we should be a witness for the Lord. We value the fellowship of Christian believers in loving community, gifted service, mutual encouragement and with godly leadership as representative of the presence of Christ on earth to meet the real needs of people *(Matt. 28:19-20; Acts 1:8; Acts 2:41-47)*.

WORSHIP

We affirm that every person is called to glorify the living God completely, freely, and passionately by giving their lives in authentic relationship, their resources in responsible stewardship, and their devotion in faithful discipleship *(Jn. 4:23-24)*.

PRAYER

We believe in communication with God and availability to God to do God's will in the earth. We believe that we must go to God with our heart and come away with His *(Matt.6)*.

About the Author

Gail E. Dudley

"...bringing you closer to Christ."

Gail Dudley is a native of Columbus, Ohio and a committed Christian focused on preparing believers for meaningful ministry. With a prayer calling upon her life, she has found great joy in leading others to pray by hosting 24-hour prayer gatherings, written books on prayer, and national prayer calls. Gail is an accomplished conference and workshop speaker who has been privileged to present the Gospel in Canada, England, South Africa, and Zimbabwe, equipping and motivating women around the world to walk boldly into their promised future. Gail is the author of seven books and many other training resources, and is the Editor-in-Chief for *READY* Publication, an edgy, different, and content-rich quarterly magazine. She has previously worked as the Vice President of Diversity for an international women's ministry and now continues to serve faithfully as a partner in ministry with The Church at North Pointe. Gail is married to Kevin and the loving mother of Alexander and Dominiq.

Booking Information

Contact Gail at <u>info.gaildudley@gmail.com</u> to schedule her for your upcoming retreat, conference, workshop, or for your book club discussion.

Other Books by Gail

*Ready to Change My Name ~
A Spiritual Journey from Fear to Faith*

*Ready to Pray ~
A Spiritual Journey of Praise and Worship*

*Ready to Pray, A Workbook ~
A Spiritual Journey of Praise and Worship*

Ready to Pray (30 Minute Prayer CD)

Transparent Moments of Gail Dudley

*Who Told You That? ~
The Truth Behind the Lies*

*Who Told You That? ~
The Truth Behind the Lies
Bible Study*

ORDER ADDITIONAL COPIES TODAY

Gail E. Dudley
www.GailDudley.com

Name: _____

Address: _____

City: _____ State: _____ Zip: _____

E-mail: _____

Would you like to join our mailing list? ❏ Yes ❏ No thank you.
Telephone: (_____) _____ - _____

Ready to Change My Name	qty: _____	($15.00 each + $2.50 S & H)
Ready to Pray (the Book)	qty: _____	($15.00 each + $2.50 S & H)
Ready to Pray (215-page Workbook)	qty: _____	($24.95 each + $3.50 S & H)
Ready to Pray (30-Minute Prayer CD)	qty: _____	($7.00 each + $2.50 S & H)
Who Told You That?	qty: _____	($17.50 each + $3.00 S & H)
Who Told You That? Bible Study	qty: _____	($17.95 each + $3.00 S & H)
Transparent Moments	qty: _____	($7.00 each + $3.00 S & H)

Book Total: $ _____ **S & H Total:** _____ **= Grand Total $** _____

Number of books being shipped: _____

Please make checks payable to:
Gail E. Dudley

Send payment to:
1491 Polaris Pkwy, Suite 81, Columbus, OH 43240
Please allow two (2) weeks for shipping

www.ingramcontent.com/pod-product-compliance
Lightning Source LLC
Chambersburg PA
CBHW060201050426
42446CB00013B/2934